The Hidden Heart Series
"Feelings"

Copyright © 2013 by Cindy Dahl
All rights reserved
www.cindydahl2007.wordpress.com

Art by Shaun Crum

ISBN : 978-1-941030-01-1

FEELINGS

By Cindy Dahl

Illustrated By Shaun Crum

Hi, I am a GLÍCK. You say it like /glēk/.
It stands for Giving, Loving, Inspiring, Caring and Kind. My books will show you how to be a GLÍCK just like me!
I have hidden a heart in one of the pages; see if you can find the love in this book.

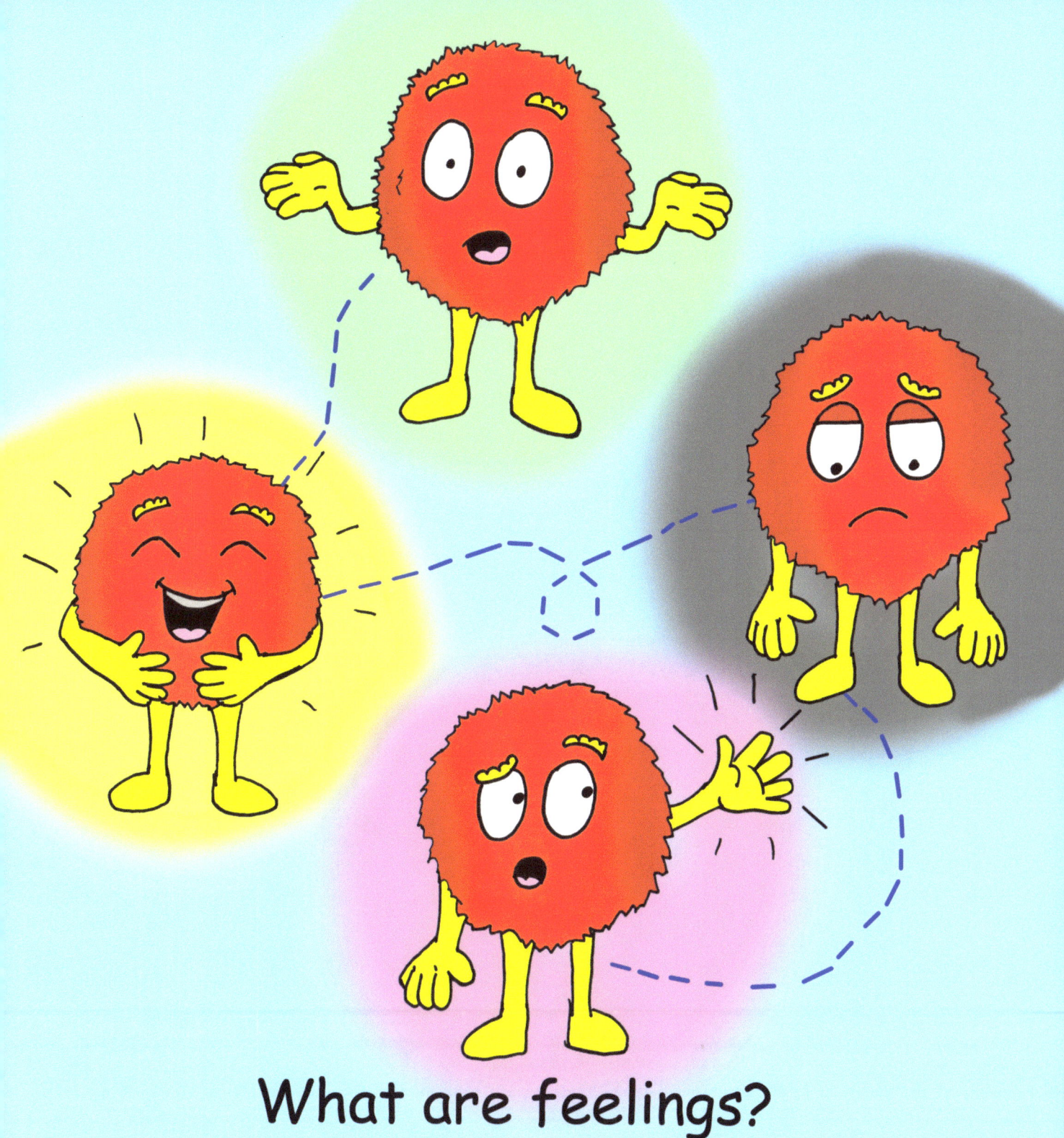

What are feelings?
And why do I have them?
What makes me giggle,
or mope or spasm?

When I am HAPPY
I like to smile.
I feel like laughing
And giggling a while.

Happy is fun.
It makes me feel light.
Happy is great
And makes things alright.

Happy is like kisses
From my favorite dog.
Or running or dancing
Or catching a frog.

When I am happy
Other people see,
And want to be happy
Just like me!

Sad can be ok
But just for a bit.
I get my favorite toy
And quietly sit.

When people see me sad
They ask me why.
I can't always tell them
But I sure do try.

I don't like being mad.
I try not to be for long.
It always helps me
To hear a good song.

When I am mad
People stay away.
I don't think they like it,
But they don't really say.

Zip, Bam, Boom
Zweedle Da Dee,
When I'm EXCITED
This happens to me!

I like being excited
By far best of all.
Being excited is great
And makes me feel tall.

I like being excited
When I get to swing.
When I run, kick a ball,
Or eat cake and ice cream.

When I am excited
It seems to be catching.
Other people get excited
Then it looks like we're matching.

Whooooooo, it's a ghost
Or a monster under my bed.
That makes me SCARED.
Is it all in my head?

When I am scared
I feel all alone.
The chills even go
Right to my bones.

My teeth might chatter
And my hands might shake.
When I am scared
My whole body might ache.

When I get to help
And I do a good job,
It makes me feel useful,
Not a bump on a log.

I did something good
Or I learned something new.
I get proud of myself
And my family does too.

So these are our feelings
That all of us have,
And I like my feelings
The good ones and bad.

Whether I'm happy
Excited or mad.
Proud of myself,
Scared or sad.

I will always have feelings
And now that I know,
I will try to stay happy
Wherever I go!

"The best and most beautiful things in the world cannot be seen or even touched. They must be felt with the heart"

— Helen Keller

Cindy Dahl is the author of several feel good children's books including the entire "hidden heart series" where kids get to find the hidden heart in each book. "It's like finding the love in the pages of a book." Cindy's main goal with writing her books is to inspire and bring a positive message for kids at a very young age. "It is never too young to learn to be kind to one another, to feel good about yourself, and to share with others."

Cindy grew up on a farm in Northern California and currently resides in Colorado. Cindy has three grown children. She read to them often when they were young and loved watching their faces when they felt the story come alive. In her spare time, Cindy enjoys being in the great Colorado outdoors.

www.ingramcontent.com/pod-product-compliance
Lightning Source LLC
Chambersburg PA
CBHW040017050426
42451CB00002B/14